"Top notch legal firm! If it wasn't for Mr. Plappert and his team at Florida Legal Advocacy Group, I have no doubt we would have lost our home. They will dig in, research your case, and get results, all while keeping you informed of the progress every step of the way. I would use this firm again in a heartbeat. Highly recommend!"

—BCB, Florida

"Great people."

—Elizabeth Dawson, Florida

"Wonderful staff and very understanding for seriously stressed-out clients. Always calm and never seemed bothered by follow-up calls. Glad to have them on my side."

—Heather Livengood, Florida

TESTIMONIALS

"During my trial this group was very professional and made it very
and comforting during this trying time for me and my family's life.
Plappert was very aggressive and knew how to win our case. I want
thank the Florida Legal Advocacy Group for all their hard work a
help and a job well done. They put the right players in place for the
and we settled two days before the trial for the amount we were aski

—James Michael Wicker, Flo

"I was in a very bad car crash that involved four cars. Attorney
Plappert helped me every step of the way and continues to
be there for me. I recovered damages from all the negligent
drivers, and he continues to pursue the case against the
insurance company for the uninsured motorist benefits."

—Michael Bartek, Flor

"Mr. Plappert is a fine and gifted attorney. I would highly recommer
him to get the job done. My previous attorney was leaving his
practice and recommended Stan Plappert to take over the case. He
had a grasp of the issues that were dragging through the courts for
almost ten years. Mr. Plappert promptly got it into the court system
for trial and we won every decision and I was completely vindicated
in every area. My only regret was not finding them sooner."

—LG, The Villages, Flori

"Great staff, excellent service!"

—Tony Montana, Flori

PREPARING AND PREVAILING IN YOUR ACCIDENT CLAIM

Taking You from Your Crash to Courtroom Success

Stanley Plappert, Esquire

Clovercroft Publishing

Preparing and Prevailing in Your Accident Claim

©2019 by Stan Plappert

Published by Clovercroft Publishing, Franklin, Tennessee

Edited by Adept Content Solutions

Cover Design by Suzanne Lawing

Interior Design by Adept Content Solutions

Printed in the United States of America

978-1-950892-12-9

Contents

Forewords

This book reveals information about the insurance industry that will surprise most attorneys and accident victims. As an insurance executive located in Sarasota, Florida and the former president of the Chartered Property and Casualty Underwriters Society, a society of over 20,000 professional insurance practitioners that have achieved the esteemed CPCU designation, this book provides insights only apparent to those like Mr. Plappert who are closest to the issues.

Being an insurance executive, I appreciate Mr. Plappert's knowledge of insurance and the law. I have worked with him throughout the years and find him to be the most knowledgeable agent and attorney that I have come to know.

Mr. Plappert and I met over seven years ago. In that time, I have witnessed his transition from insurance to law. His determination to help his clients and share his understanding is admirable.

I have never met an attorney with the comprehension that Mr. Plappert has in the insurance industry. I believe you will enjoy this book and the personal injury advice he offers here and through his other media sources.

Michael Koscielny
Past President of the Chartered Property and
Casualty Underwriters Society
Sarasota, Florida

As a business law teaching professor and an attorney, I know the qualities to look for in other attorneys when providing referrals or seeking advice. I have known Stanley Plappert since 1995, and he is a very knowledgeable—I would even say brilliant—person. I knew Stanley when he was a partner with a large commercial insurance agency in Northern Indiana.

Mr. Plappert is a very competitive and aggressive attorney, which is why I feel confident in referring potential clients to him. His aggressive yet professional approach in litigation matters frequently results in positive results for his clients. He stands behind his promises and strictly adheres to the ethics required of an attorney.

I recommend this book to any person interested in knowing the perspective of an insurance agent and attorney in a personal injury case, as Mr. Plappert is both. He has experience that is unique to the legal field, which makes him a great personal injury attorney.

James A. O'Brien, Esquire
Attorney and Teaching Professor
South Bend, Indiana

For over a decade I have known Stan Plappert on a personal and professional basis. As an entrepreneur involved in several business ventures I am constantly seeking out professional advice. And because of Mr. Plappert's experience and expertise, my family has relied on him to help us navigate through several insurance and legal matters.

As friends, our personal paths cross weekly in my hometown of Belleview where we attend church together. And it is here where I regularly witness Mr. Plappert interacting with many other individuals as he also helps them through legal and personal injury challenges.

Some of the defining traits Stan is known for are his confidence and aggressiveness in how he approaches his cases. He is uniquely qualified to write this book, and for those needing advice in these matters you will come to realize quickly that you have found a solution.

Ryan D. Chamberlin

Ryan Chamberlin
Best Selling Author, Speaker and Entrepreneur
Belleview, Florida

Preface

This project is a result of several years of encouragement by family, friends, and clients in an effort to memorialize some of my training and expertise for the benefit of the general public. This would not have happened without the assistance of many people, especially my associate, Ashley Broussard, and proofreader, Angel Craig. I am thankful for the patience of my staff and my family throughout the entire process.

Introduction

Most of my life has been dedicated to the insurance industry and legal field. I have gained insightful knowledge that I provide to my clients on a regular basis. After bringing closure and recovering damages for many injured victims, I decided to write this book to help accident victims that I may never meet in person.

This book is intended to help victims of an accident by providing useful tips and methods for recovering damages. It is a general personal injury guide and does not replace hiring an attorney for specific advice pertaining to your case.

Chapter One
The Crash

An automobile accident is a very traumatic experience and may cause lifelong suffering. It is not always the injuries themselves that cause the suffering; it may be the memories of the accident and the loss of others involved. There are many ways that an accident can affect you.

Your life may change in a split second after being in an accident. I have met numerous accident victims throughout the years who suffered permanent injuries. The victims have been my close friends, members of my church, and clients. Regardless of how we meet, I feel it is my obligation to help you and other accident victims through the process.

When you are involved in an accident, the first thing you must do is make sure all parties receive the medical attention they need. Then call the police, as you will need a record of the accident. Do not admit fault for anything without first speaking to your attorney. You will be under a lot of stress and unable to think clearly at the time, so it is best to avoid making statements regarding your own fault. Be sure to inform the officer if you noticed the other driver doing something illegal, as it will be helpful to your cause if the other party receives a citation.

1

After an accident:

1. Stop vehicle

2. Seek medical attention if needed

3. Report accident

4. Do NOT admit anything

5. Obtain the witnesses information

6. Take photos

7. Contact an attorney for advice

8. Call your insurance company (or your attorney will)

9. Call other driver's insurance company (or your attorney will)

10. Get your valuables out of the vehicle prior to tow

Also, protect your identity. There is no need to provide your social security number or allow the other party to photograph your driver's license. The Department of Motor Vehicles mentions providing the other party involved in the accident with the vehicle make, model, year, color, VIN; insurance information; and your name and phone number.[1]

Regardless of how minor the damage may appear at the time of the accident, you will not know for certain until you are examined by a physician. Many people at the scene of an accident think they are okay but find out later they are not. Therefore, avoid leaving the scene of an accident without first reporting the accident to the police and obtaining a copy of the other party's insurance for your records.

Take pictures of both or all vehicles involved, including the license plates. Take inside photos of the vehicles involved if there is any inside damage. Take photos of the surroundings.

What time of day is it? What is the weather condition? These are all factors to consider, as questions may arise later. The Florida Department of Highway Safety and Motor Vehicles, or DHSMV, maintains statistics and I have included them to demonstrate times and days of week when accidents occur most often.

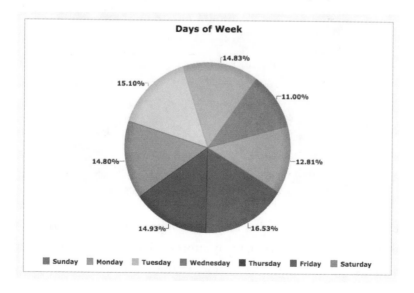

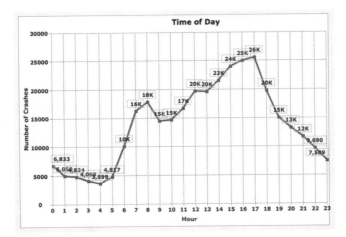

I have personally handled cases where the time of the day was a very important factor of the case.

The sun or weather condition may cause your vision to be impaired, and when this may have occurred, many attorneys including me hire an expert to demonstrate the weather conditions to the court.

Obtain the insurance information of the other parties involved. Remember: you need to know the name of the other party's insurance company, not their agent or agency. Smith Insurance Agency is not an insurance company. You need to get their insurance policy number to make reporting the claim easier.

Go get checked out right away. Go to the emergency room or local clinic the day of the accident—do not delay. You may not feel like you need to be taken away in ambulance, but you will likely not feel so good the day after the crash or the second day after. The longer you wait to seek medical treatment, the bigger deal the insurance company attorneys will make about the delay. The insurance company will try to make it look like you were not hurt in the accident but are just trying to get insurance money and take advantage of the system. They do not know how you felt at the time of the accident or the days following, but they will do their best to make you look bad to the jury.

Look at the accident scene to see if you can tell if the other driver was wearing his or her seat belt. Look and see if you can tell if they were on their phone or texting. These can be important later in the case. You need to develop a habit of always wearing your seat belt and never texting while you drive. These habits will save your life and help your case if you are ever involved in accident.

Ask questions of the other driver if you can: Were they on the job? Where were they heading? Ask them where they came from. See if you can smell alcohol or drugs on them. If you do, report it to the police when they arrive.

Be careful about using social media, and be careful what you text or email to your friends and family about the crash, your injuries, and your activities after the crash. All—and I repeat, all—of your social media are discoverable to the other side in a personal injury case. It is not uncommon for people to post after a crash, "I am thankful I was just in a car crash and I am not injured." How will that sound to a jury when you are telling them how bad you are hurt, how wrong the other driver was, and how this has disrupted your life. First of all, you may not know the extent of your injuries for a few days, so do not post anything on social media about your crash or your injuries, ever.

You can call your family and your good friends and tell them you were involved in a crash and you do not yet know the severity of any injuries, but you are alive and hopeful for a full recovery. Please, just be very careful not to say or do anything that will hurt your case later. Anything you say or do will be used against you, I promise. This may not be fair, but it is how things work.

In addition to your current social media post being used against you, there are times where your prior postings may be discoverable by the defendant. Therefore, the images and other posts will not be protected once you file suit. Generally, the postings are neither privileged nor protected by any right of privacy, regardless of any privacy settings.[2]

The recent case of *Nucci* is an example of where the court held the plaintiff's social media posts were discoverable, meaning the defendant could obtain copies.[3] In this case, the court found the photos from two years prior to the accident until the time of accident were reasonably calculated to discoverable evidence in the personal injury case.[4] I have personally handled cases where the defendant's attorney would ask for social media passwords and other account information.

The text from the *Nucci* case follows, to provide you an example, where the court ordered the images from social media to be produced.

1. For each social networking account listed in response to the interrogatories, please ***provide copies or screenshots of all photographs associated with that account during the two (2) years prior to the date of loss.***

2. For each social networking account listed in the interrogatories, provide ***copies or screenshots of all photographs associated with that account from the date of loss to present.***

3. For each cell phone listed in the interrogatories, please provide ***copies or screenshots of all photographs associated with that account during the two years prior to the date of loss.***

4. For each cellular phone listed in response to the interrogatories, please provide *copies or screenshots of all photographs associated with that account from the date of loss to present.*

5. For each cellular phone listed in the interrogatories, please provide *copies of any documentation outlining what calls were made or received on the date of loss.*

Florida evidence rules apply to all cases brought in state court. Although this case involved a slip-and-fall matter, the court would view evidence to determine damages in an automobile accident the same way. The *Nucci* case is a good example of how social media photos can be viewed and used against you. Any and all photos and cameras, whether they are recovered from a street camera, store camera, or even an ATM machine camera, may be used against you. Be careful.

After the accident, many people may tell you their accident stories and instruct you on ways to handle your insurance company and the other party. Although these people may provide you great advice, every case is different, and the type of damages you have may be significantly different. As previously mentioned, it is in your best interest to avoid giving out too much information without first seeking legal help.

The idea of representing yourself in court may seem frightening, and it is for many people. Moreover, the time you would invest in preparing the case and litigating it may affect your work and personal life. When an attorney properly handles the case, it sometimes leads to an early settlement where you can recover your damages and avoid trial. If it does go to trial, the attorney has worked on your case for months and is well prepared to explain your injuries to a judge and jury.

When the case is concluded, the attorney will be able to negotiate medical reductions on your behalf and potentially save you money on outstanding bills that resulted from the accident. When you represent yourself, these tasks may be more difficult and not lead to the best possible result.

Chapter Two

Two Threshold Issues

The first threshold issue is fault. With the help of your attorney, you must determine who was at fault in the accident. You should notify the officer at the scene if the party did something that was illegal or you noticed the smell of alcohol. If one party received a citation for the accident, they are most likely at fault.

The issuance of a citation is not certain fault, but it is a good indicator. Please keep in mind the citation is not admissible in trial unless it is used as evidence of perjury, forgery, falsification, uttering, or as physical evidence of the citation.[5]

VIOLATIONS				
PERSON #	NAME OF VIOLATOR	FL STATUTE NUMBER	CHARGE	CITATION NUMBER
1		316.075(1C1)	FAILED TO STOP AT STEADY RED LIGHT	
PERSON #	NAME OF VIOLATOR	FL STATUTE NUMBER	CHARGE	CITATION NUMBER
PERSON #	NAME OF VIOLATOR	FL STATUTE NUMBER	CHARGE	CITATION NUMBER

HSMV 90010 S (V) (rev 10/10)   Page _2_ of _7_

There is also the rebuttable presumption of fault in rear-end accidents; therefore, the party that rear-ends another is usually found liable for the other party's damages unless proven otherwise.[6] For example, in the case of *Servello & Sons, Inc. v. Sims,* Sims's automobile became disabled and was stalled in the road.[7] Sims attempted to self-tow and, after the auto disconnected from the vehicle hauling it, Sims left it in the middle of the road and attempted to reattach it to the front vehicle. Sims did not make an effort to push the vehicle off the road, nor did they place cones or lights to warn the oncoming traffic.[8] The defendant crashed into the back of the parked car.[9] The court found the defendant was not presumed at fault although defendant rear-ended front car because of the evidence provided.[10]

Generally, the party rear-ended may argue that the driver behind his or her vehicle is at fault; however, the driver that struck the automobile in front of it may provide evidence to rebut the allegation of negligence.

The Florida court will consider all evidence and apply comparative negligence. If the case goes to trial and is heard by a jury, the lawyers will agree on jury instructions and a verdict form that will be approved by the judge. The jury instructions and the verdict form will look similar to ones I have attached at the end of this book. Reviewing the jury instructions and verdict form will provide you valuable insight about the important elements of your case that the judge and jury will consider.

The facts of the circumstances regarding what caused the accident are what determines fault. If the case goes to trial, the jury will determine which party is at fault. The simple issue is who caused the accident or who was in the wrong. If it is determined that you are the at fault party, your insurance company will appoint a defense attorney to represent you.

It is important to take photos of any rear-end damage that may have occurred to your vehicle and, if you rear-ended the other party, be sure to take photos of your surroundings.

Remember, we are in an era of technology, and most people have camera phones; therefore, other people at the scene of the accident may also take photographs of the accident.

Obtain contact information of as many witnesses as possible. Write down the names, addresses, and phone numbers of any possible witnesses to the accident. The defenses to the rear-end presumption in Florida are determined on a case-by-case basis.[11]

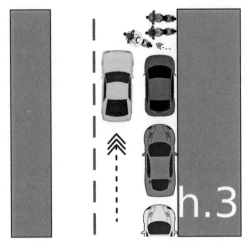

Gathering the aforementioned information may help your case. A sample of the witness portion of the accident report follows. Please make sure you obtain a copy of the report for your records and to bring to your attorney.

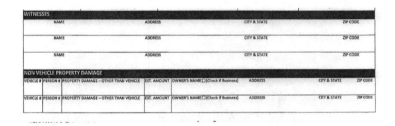

The second threshold issue is whether the "at fault" party has insurance coverage to pay for your damages. Your attorney will likely request a copy of the policy after the consultation to review the "at fault" party's coverage. Also, your policy will be reviewed to determine if you carry an optional coverage known as "Uninsured Motorist" Liability Insurance coverage, which covers its insured when the responsible party does not have enough coverage to pay for your losses. When the responsible party does not have enough insurance coverage to pay your damages, your Uninsured Motorist Liability Insurance coverage, also known as UM coverage, will allow you to recover the amount from your insurance company.

In summation, the party at fault and the insurance coverage are the two main issues that you and your attorney must first consider. The accident report, witnesses, and photographs will help determine the party at fault. The insurance policies of both you and the other party will provide the limits and determine if there is sufficient coverage for your damages. After fault and coverage is determined, then you and your attorney may or may not decide to proceed and file suit against the other party or parties.

Chapter Three
Attorney Inquiry

Most people want to know what they should consider when hiring an attorney. Start your search by looking for an attorney licensed in the state where the accident occurred and who is experienced in the area of law in which you need representation.

You want an attorney who will fight for your case and obtain the best recovery possible. The insurance companies know which attorneys they prefer to settle cases with versus fighting in a trial. Some of the questions that may help you decide if the attorney is best for you are as follows:

1. What type of cases does your firm handle?

2. Have you ever had a case like mine (automobile, motorcycle, golf cart, etc.)?

    a. If so, what was the outcome of the case?

3. Have you ever been to trial?

4. Will you take my case to trial if necessary?

5. What experience do you have in personal injury that differs from other attorneys?

There are many attorneys in Florida who handle personal injury cases. We see billboards along the highway advertising legal help to accident victims. However, not many appear to have experience on the other side of the field—the insurance industry. In addition to being an attorney, insurance industry experience is what makes the attorney understand the views and arguments that may arise during litigation. I am an attorney who has played both sides of the field and knows what to expect.

My first full-time job out of college was working for an insurance company. The job was as a regional representative for Church Mutual Insurance selling insurance to churches and nursing homes in western Illinois. The position gave me the experience of measuring buildings and preparing replacement cost estimates. After working for Church Mutual for five years, all it took was a drive up to a church to be able to estimate the replacement value of the building within ten percent before leaving the car. My next job was working for an independent agency in Indiana. As independent agents, we represented many different insurance companies and could choose the company that best met the needs of clients as opposed to a captive insurance agent, who only represents one insurance company.

A little bit of free advice that has nothing to do with your crash or personal injury law: I strongly recommend you have an independent agent. You will be better represented by professionals who have your best interest at heart, especially if you can find a Trusted Choice agent.

My book of business included many companies and individuals in Northern Indiana and Southern Michigan at my time working for Gibson Insurance. An important ingredient in my success was studying insurance to be the best in my career, including enrolling in graduate level insurance programs and receiving my Chartered Property and Casualty Underwriter (CPCU) designation. Many believe this is the highest level of education achievement you can attain the property and casualty insurance world.

Other professional designations achieved in my insurance career include the Chartered Life Underwriter (CLU), Charter Financial Consultant (ChFC), Associate in Risk Management (ARM), and Associate in Marine Insurance Management (AMIM). In other words, I was a real insurance nerd, which allowed me to explain and design coverages for my clients as well or better than anyone.

Why is this background part of this book? Because my insurance background allows me to think and act differently than other personal injury attorneys. Personal injury cases are mostly about the insurance. Very few cases are brought against defendants who have no insurance. Most people who have no insurance have no assets. That is not always the case, but it is the case over 99 percent of the time. So in reality, personal injury law is about obtaining the most favorable settlement for the client from the insurance company, whether through negotiation or a jury verdict.

My background is unique, and few, if any other personal injury attorneys, have similar experience. I understand that many insurance adjusters get bonuses for paying out a lower amount of claims. No insurance company chastises their adjusters for giving out too little on a personal injury claim. Most claims are valued at 10 percent to 20 percent of their real value by the adjuster, until it gets close to time for the trial.

Insurance accounting for reserves is an important business management function for insurance executives. If the insurance company has to increase a reserve for your case, it comes out of the operating profit, and if they can lower a reserve, it goes right into their operating income.

Most agents also receive a contingency commission if their book of business is profitable—in other words, if their clients have fewer claims and smaller claims. Everyone on the insurance side is incentivized to pay you less money. These are facts that not everyone knows.

The person who caused the accident is the at-fault party. Sometimes it is easy to tell who is at fault and sometimes it is not. NEVER admit that an accident is your fault. DO NOT tell the other party that you are sorry. Check on the other party and make sure they are okay, make sure they get medical help, be nice, be friendly, but DO NOT say that you are sorry or that you were at fault.

If you decide to hire an attorney to represent you, there is information you should discuss with your attorney and items you may want to bring to the initial meeting or soon thereafter. I have provided a list below to help you for your meeting.

1. Accident report

2. Insurance policy

3. Medical bills

4. Physicians' names who are treating you

5. Correspondence between you and other parties

6. Witnesses information

7. Expenses that resulted from accident

8. Photographs from accident scene

9. Photographs of injuries

10. Citations/legal notices

11. Any notes/journal with notes to help your case

Chapter Four

Determining Fault

The legal term we use for fault is *negligence*. Fault or negligence can be established by a violation of right of way. When one party has a right of way to enter an intersection and the other party enters that intersection instead, they have violated the right of way. The violation of a law can sometimes be used to establish negligence. In addition, the violation of an industry standard can also be used.

Let me caution you that although a police citation may be issued to the at fault party, a citation in and of itself does not determine negligence or liability for a personal injury. All of the facts of the case have to weighed, and sometimes the party that was not issued the citation is the at-fault party.

In addition, you should know that police citations and reports are not admissible into evidence and cannot be discussed at a trial for a personal injury case in the State of Florida.[12] In the case of *Sottilaro,* the court found the statement made in the accident report was admissible to impeach a witness. It further held the privilege that excludes accident reports from evidence in Florida is to protect the parties against self-incrimination and not to exclude statements made by non-party witnesses.[13] This being said, it is evident how important the witnesses' statements can be in a trial.

Please make sure you ask witnesses for their information before they leave the scene of an accident.

There is a rebuttable presumption of fault in rear-end accidents.[14] The party that rear-ends another is usually found liable for the other party's damages unless proven otherwise.[15] Even when both parties are negligent and liable for the injuries caused, Florida allows recovery under comparative negligence, as discussed in other chapters in more detail.

Remember we have to deal with facts and evidence, not just what you thought at the time. Also, it is important to understand that your facts and evidence will be presented in the context of the law to a jury of your peers. Much of establishing fault or negligence is good old-fashioned common sense. Once you have established fault or negligence, then we need to examine the possibility of comparative negligence, which is covered in a later chapter.

In many cases the fault is clear, and the insurance company will admit fault but dispute damages. A low percentage of cases go to trial to determine fault; most go to trial to determine damages. In the United States, only four to five percent of the personal injury cases go to trial, and of those cases, approximately 95 percent are settled during pretrial stages.[16] I always advise my clients to bring their case to trial when it is in their best interest. However, if the settlement offer meets their demand and I strongly believe going to trial will not be beneficial to my client, then I advise settling the matter early and saving their time and costs.

Chapter Five

Types of Accidents

Many examples used in this book are about car crashes because those are the most common crashes that create personal injury claims, but in Central Florida golf carts are a very common cause of personal injury claims. Truck crashes are not as common as car crashes but can be much more severe and require a special expertise. Motorcycle crashes have catastrophic potential, and often because car drivers do not pay enough attention to motorcycles on the road, they often cause these crashes and accompanying severe injuries. Bicycle and pedestrian accidents also can give rise to personal injury claims. Each of these types of crashes will be addressed in this chapter.

		2016	2015	2014	% Change 2015 to 2016	3 Year Average
General Statistics	Total Crashes	395,785	374,342	344,170	5.73%	371,432
	Drivers Involved	668,699	630,550	581,090	6.05%	626,780
	Average Crashes per Day	1,081	1,025	943	5.46%	1,016
	Mileage Death Rate (per 100 million VMT)	1.48	1.42	1.24	4.23%	1.38
	Fatal Crashes	2,935	2,699	2,336	8.74%	2,657
	Fatalities	3,176	2,939	2,494	8.06%	2,870
	Injury Crashes	165,940	159,795	149,426	3.85%	158,387
	Injuries	254,155	243,316	225,608	4.45%	241,026
	Incapacitating Injury Crashes	17,568	17,545	16,967	0.13%	17,360
	Incapacitating Injuries	21,645	21,546	20,907	0.46%	21,366
	Property Damage Only	226,910	211,848	192,408	7.11%	210,389

		2016	2015	2014	% Change 2015 to 2016	3 Year Average
Vulnerable Road Users	Motorcycle Crashes	10,331	10,201	9,854	1.27%	10,129
	Motorcycle Fatalities	515	546	427	-5.68%	496
	Motorcycle Injuries	8,256	8,231	8,040	0.30%	8,176
	Motorcycle Passenger Fatalities	30	38	22	-21.05%	30
	Motorcycle Passenger Injuries	742	814	809	-8.85%	788
	Pedestrian Crashes	9,102	9,085	8,838	0.19%	9,008
	Pedestrian Fatalities	667	632	606	5.54%	635
	Pedestrian Injuries	7,796	7,870	7,737	-0.94%	7,801
	Bicycle Crashes	6,668	7,120	7,077	-6.35%	6,955
	Bicyclist Fatalities	140	154	135	-9.09%	143
	Bicyclist Injuries	6,234	6,691	6,680	-6.83%	6,535
	Other Non-Motorist Crashes	2,038	2,330	2,516	-12.53%	2,295
	Other Non-Motorist Fatalities	5	16	9	-68.75%	10
	Other Non-Motorist Injuries	371	367	399	1.09%	379

Source: Florida's Integrated Report Exchange System (FIRES) database located at the following: https://firesportal.com/Pages/Public/DHSMVPublishedDocuments/Most%20Recent%20Year/Crash%20 Facts%202016.pdf

Car crashes are pretty straightforward and used in most of our examples in this book. Issues with car crashes are driver actions, driver capabilities, driver distractions, and driver use of alcohol or drugs. Many of these factors apply to other types of crashes as well. In a car accident the condition of the car can be an issue as can use of the safety equipment.

BUCKLE UP! WEAR YOUR SEATBELT!

It is important that you always use your seat belt; that will be an issue if the other party was at fault. The lack of use of your seat belt could greatly decrease your recovery and make your case much more difficult. Your driving record may come into play, and your past use of drugs may also be an issue.

Truck accidents are usually much more severe than car crashes because of the weight and size of the vehicle involved. There are many additional regulations for truck drivers and that means many more issues have to be investigated. Almost every truck has a black box that records all of the vehicle information just prior to the crash and during the crash including the speed, braking action, and so on.

Truck drivers are required to maintain time logs that may be pertinent. Often truck drivers will be required to undergo drug and alcohol testing at the crash scene or soon thereafter. An engineering expert needs to be called out right away to inspect the vehicles and gather information. So, if you are involved a truck crash, get medical treatment first, but call an attorney right away. Time is of the essence.

Golf carts are a very common mode transportation in Central Florida, especially in a certain planned community. There are two types of commonly used vehicles: the golf cart and the LSV, or low speed vehicle. Golf carts cannot exceed 20 mph, do not have safety equipment such as safety belts or headlights as standard equipment, and do not require license plates in the State of Florida. Low Speed Vehicles look like golf carts and are often called golf carts. LSVs can go up to 35 mph, have seat belts and headlights, and must be registered and have license plates.

The determination of fault or negligence is made in the same method as with car crashes. Golf cart crashes can be very severe and can cause catastrophic injuries. If you are involved in a crash involving a golf cart or LSV, get medical treatment right away and contact a qualified attorney. The other party may be responsible for repairing or replacing your golf cart or LSV. They may also be responsible for your injuries and other damages.

Motorcycle accidents are more commonly caused by a larger vehicle. The driver of a larger vehicle may be distracted, underestimate the speed of the motorcycle, or fail to obey traffic signs, among numerous other possibilities. When it comes to motorcycle accidents, you can be severely impaired. My associate personally knows an individual with nerve damage who is permanently disabled after a motorcycle accident that occurred outside of Florida. Unfortunately, the defendant's insurance coverage did not allow him to recover as much as he needed.

Keep in mind, Personal Injury Protection, known as PIP, is not available on motorcycles in Florida, and your auto PIP will not cover you while on a motorcycle.[17] The rules also differ according to age. Persons over 21 may ride without a helmet but must have a minimum of $10,000 coverage in health insurance or medical coverage.[18] Motorcycle drivers under the age of 21 must wear a helmet.[19] Since a majority of motorcycle accidents involve a larger vehicle, it is highly recommended that you wear a helmet regardless of age. This will protect you and further prevent the negligent party from alleging you are partially or wholly at fault for your own injuries.

Bicycle accidents occur more often than most of us know. Florida's fatalities have been among the highest in the nation. In 2015, Florida had 150 bicycle fatal accidents. The next closest state was California with 129.[20] There are several reasons for the high number of bicycle accidents. The driver of the automobile may be negligent, or the bicyclist may be negligent. The following charts from the Statewide Analysis of Bicycle Crashes Report prepared for the Research Center Florida Department of Transportation show the acts and injuries associated with the accidents studied. There is a list of bicycle safety tips at the end of this book.

Action Prior to the Crash	Bicyclist Fatalities	Bicyclist Injuries	Uninjured Bicyclists	Total Bicyclists[1]	Proportion of Total Bicyclists
Crossing Roadway	209	7,845	1,055	9,303	35.2%
Waiting to Cross Roadway	7	274	54	343	1.3%
Cycling Along Roadway with Traffic	153	4,277	427	4,930	18.6%
Cycling Along Roadway against Traffic	35	1,887	263	2,214	8.4%
Cycling on Sidewalk	24	5,034	693	5,857	22.1%
In Roadway (working, playing, etc.)	20	474	63	573	2.2%
Adjacent to Roadway	15	300	43	367	1.4%
Going to or from School	0	143	22	168	0.6%
Working in Traffic Way	0	1	1	2	0.0%
None	5	233	32	275	1.0%
Other	23	1,485	277	1,831	6.9%
Unknown	14	432	149	599	2.3%
Total	**505**	**22,385**	**3,079**	**26,462**	**100.0%**

[1] Total bicyclists include bicyclists with unknown severity and non-traffic fatalities.

Bicyclist's Location at the Time of the Crash	Bicyclist Fatalities	Bicyclist Injuries	Uninjured Bicyclists	Total Bicyclists[1]
Intersection[2]	137 (1.2%)	9,882 (85.5%)	1,321 (11.4%)	11,563 (100%)
Segment[3]	305 (2.8%)	9,260 (84.9%)	1,198 (11.0%)	10,910 (100%)
Driveway/Access	4 (0.3%)	1,184 (83.9%)	163 (11.5%)	1,412 (100%)
Shared-use Path or Trail	2 (1.9%)	91 (85.8%)	8 (7.5%)	106 (100%)
Non-traffic Way Area	1 (1.6%)	46 (74.2%)	13 (21.0%)	62 (100%)
Other	44 (2.4%)	1,515 (81.5%)	252 (13.6%)	1,859 (100%)
Unknown	12 (2.2%)	407 (74.0%)	124 (22.5%)	550 (100%)
Total	**505 (1.9%)**	**22,385 (84.6%)**	**3,079 (11.6%)**	**26,462 (100%)**

[1] Total bicyclists include bicyclists with unknown severity and non-traffic fatalities.
[2] Intersection location includes crashes that occurred at intersection-marked crosswalk, intersection-unmarked crosswalk, intersection-other locations.
[3] Segment location includes crashes that occurred at midblock-marked crosswalk, travel lane-other location, bicycle lane, shoulder/roadside, sidewalk, and median/crossing island.

Source: Statewide Analysis of Bicycle Crashes located at:
http://www.fdot.gov/research/Completed_Proj/Summary_SF/FDOT-BDV29–977–23-rpt.pdf

In another study, motorists were found to be at fault in more crashes than bicyclists; however, fatalities were more often caused by mistakes made by the bicyclist.[21] This is why following the proper safety procedures is important. Although, Florida will allow recovery from the negligent party even if you are partially liable for your own injuries, the goal is preventing injuries and death.

Keep in mind, riding at night and against the traffic is more dangerous than daytime bicycling and riding with the traffic. Stay in your own lane and wear a helmet with bicycle reflectors.

Pedestrians face similar dangers as bicyclists. There is less protection for pedestrians and bicyclist than riding in an automobile. Drivers of an automobile have many distractions on the road, especially if they are on their phone. It is important to avoid walking in the road and to stay on the sidewalks. Walking or running on the sidewalk provides some space between you and the driver of the automobile. Look and listen! Keep your headphones off or on a low volume so that you may listen for automobiles. Keep your dog on a leash. Wear reflectors in the evening. Do what you can to avoid being injured.

The following chart contains the 2018 statistics regarding all types of accidents in Florida to date.

Crash Summary	
Total Crashes:	334,514
Injury Crashes:	138,947
Total Injuries:	212,090
Crashes with Traffic Fatalities:	2,292
Total Traffic Fatalities	2,459
Commercial Vehicle Crashes:	37,702
Commercial Vehicles:	40,746
Property Damage Crashes:	193,275
*Pedestrian Crashes:	7,537
*Pedestrian Fatalities:	544
**Bicycle Crashes:	5,539
**Bicycle Fatalities:	110

As of Date: 11/11/2018

Regardless, if you are riding a bicycle, walking, running, skipping, or hopping and are struck by a vehicle, seek medical attention immediately. Do not assume everything is okay, as you may later realize you were in shock and were, in fact, injured.

Chapter Six

Insurance Coverage

This chapter will discuss the type of insurance policy that would best protect you in an accident and how to prepare for such an unfortunate situation. Please be sure to understand your insurance coverage and keep a copy of your insurance card in your automobile. Also, update your emergency contacts associated with your driver's license.

Florida requires that every person with a registered vehicle in Florida and those who are in Florida more than 90 days out of the last 365 days carry the minimum insurance. The minimum limits and types of insurance in Florida are as follows: Personal Injury Protection and Property Damage in the amounts of $10,000 each; Bodily Injury in the amount of $10,000.[22]

In Florida, Personal Injury Protection (PIP) is available regardless of fault because Florida is a "no fault state." Your automobile insurance will not increase by using your PIP coverage when you not the party at fault.[23] PIP covers 80 percent to 100 percent (depending on what you purchase) of all necessary and reasonable medical expenses that resulted from the accident regardless of fault.[24] However, the initial treatment must be within 14 days of the accident, and there are limits to the coverage.[25] If the treatment is for nonemergency medical, then there is a limit of $2,500, and if it is for emergency medical, then there is a limit of $10,000 unless a greater policy amount was purchased.[26] Bodily Injury (BI) protects you from injuries or death you cause to another and are found legally liable for. Although these required coverages may not cover the damages that occur from an incident, there are other optional coverages such as Uninsured Motorists Liability Insurance, also known as UM coverage. Here is a copy of a policy with UM coverage.

Coverages*	Limits and/or Deductibles
Bodily Injury Liability	
Each Person/Each Occurrence	$50,000/$100,000
Property Damage Liability	$100,000
Personal Injury Protection	$500 Ded/Insd&Rel
Uninsured Motorist/Nonstacked	
Each Person/Each Occurrence	$25,000/$50,000
Comprehensive	$500 Ded
Collision	$500 Ded
Emergency Road Service	Ers Full
Rental Reimbursement	$45 Per Day
	$1,350 Max

I cannot overemphasize the importance of each person carrying Uninsured Motorists Liability Insurance and carrying as high of a limit as you can afford. Uninsured Motorists Liability Insurance provides coverage to its insured when the responsible party does not have any or enough coverage to pay for your losses.

When the responsible party does not have any or enough insurance coverage to pay your damages, your UM coverage will allow you to recover the amount from your insurance company. This coverage is advised because many drivers do not carry a policy that will cover all of your damages. Many injured clients face this issue time and time again. The clients are injured, and the responsible party had little or no coverage. When this occurs then you may have your own insurance policy cover the damages you suffered from the accident.

Chapter Seven

Comparative Negligence

In Florida, the plaintiff is not precluded from recovering damages from the defendant even when the plaintiff is partially at fault for his or her own damages.[27] The amount of damages are reduced by the plaintiff's own contribution.[28] This applies to several situations that may arise in an accident, such as, the plaintiff not wearing a seatbelt or speeding.

Many questions will arise when determining if the plaintiff was negligent, which may include some of the following: was plaintiff wearing a seatbelt, speeding, texting, or drinking, and was the accident avoidable. The insurance company may request an Examination under Oath, which is a formal proceeding where they ask questions and you cannot plead the Fifth. Similar questions will likely be asked again in later discovery. Everything you say can be used against your claim; therefore, I would suggest hiring an attorney prior to this examination and asking your attorney to be present.

For example, in the case of *Lenhart,* the plaintiff was a passenger on a scooter and was struck by the defendant, the driver of an automobile. The plaintiff was not wearing a helmet at the time of the accident and suffered permanent brain damage.[29] Although the defendant admitted fault for the collision, the court still found the negligence of both plaintiff and defendant was admissible evidence.[30] The court held it should presented to the jury to compare the totality of fault from both parties.[31]

Situations may arise where the court and jury find both the plaintiff was negligent and in some way a contributing factor. The percentage of defendant's fault is then reduced accordingly, but plaintiff is not barred so long as plaintiff was not 100 percent at fault for own injuries. Most attorneys will make every effort to convince the court and jury that the injuries would have occurred regardless of plaintiff's negligence to prevent the recoverable amount of damages from being reduced.

There are many instances where the defendant's attorney will subpoena the plaintiff's phone records and use them to allege that the plaintiff talking on the phone during the accident contributed to his or her own injuries. Most attorneys will file motions to exclude certain pieces of evidence. If the court grants the motion, then the evidence will not be admissible for the jury to hear; however, if the court denies the motion, the evidence is admissible.

In the case of *Antico,* a driver was killed in a collision and his estate sued a trucking company.[32] The defendant, the trucking company, asked the court to order the plaintiff, the deceased's estate, to provide the deceased's cell phone for inspection. The defendant wanted to view the phone history, GPS, and texts to determine whether deceased was on the phone at time of accident.[33] Although defendant already had retrieved the phone records from the cell phone provider, the court found the defendant's expert was also permitted to inspect the phone itself for relevant information.[34]

If the jury finds that talking on the phone during the accident was negligent and thus unable to avoid a collision that a person not on the phone would have been able to avoid, then you, the plaintiff, may have a reduced award. It may even be zero. Therefore, it is important to discuss all of these factors with your attorney, so he or she may prepare you for the best defense to contributing negligence.

Chapter Eight

Injuries

When you are in an accident, you should seek immediate medical attention, regardless how minor you think your injuries may be. Only a physician will know the extent of your injuries. The physician may require lab work, x-rays, an MRI, and other tests to properly diagnose you.

The physician may recommend you see another doctor who specializes in the type of injury you have. A referral to another doctor may also occur after you have reached your maximum medical improvement. This means the current doctor has improved your condition as much as possible, and you may need surgery or other procedures that another physician will need to decide.

The inability to pay for medical care immediately upon receiving it does not necessarily preclude you from treatment. Many injured plaintiffs receive treatment and the hospital and physician will place a lien on the pending suit. However, some providers will require a "letter of protection" from your attorney prior to providing you with medical care. A Letter of Protection, also referred to as an LOP, is a letter from your attorney that promises the provider will be paid at the time of settlement.

I have provided numerous LOPs to providers for my clients over the years, and it has allowed some to continue care—sometimes even surgery—that may not have been possible without the LOP. This allows you to obtain the medical attention you need and assures the medical provider payment for those services rendered.

Chapter Nine

Permanent Injury

Permanent injury is a key threshold. A permanent injury usually requires long-term care and affects your enjoyment of life. When my clients suffer from permanent injuries, we demand a significant amount more from the defendant. Although my clients may never enjoy life the way they did prior to the accident because of the injuries, it is important to make sure they are financially whole, or at least as much as is possible. The long-term medical and care expenses are some of the many damages accounted for in the demand made to the insurance company.

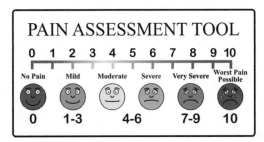

A permanency rating should be requested from the client's physician to evaluate the extent of the injuries and the possibility of recovery, if there is any possibility. I use my knowledge in personal injury and the insurance field along with the doctor's final report to determine an amount to demand from the defendant. The defendant will almost always counter a demand and argue the injuries are not permanent. Therefore, do not be discouraged by the defendant or their insurance company denying your demand and initially offering a significantly lower amount. This is part of the process, and your attorney should update you along the way when offers are made.

Chapter Ten

Previous Medical History

The insurance company will attempt to prove your injuries are preexisting. The insurance company will almost always try to make your previous medical history the issue and claim that your injuries (if they are real) are not caused by the current accident but were preexisting. All previous accidents, surgeries, and illnesses will be questioned by the defendant. Your attorney may argue that some of the preexisting conditions are not relevant to the present injuries or your attorney may argue the accident exacerbated the preexisting injuries. This will depend on your injuries, case, and attorney.

It is important that you tell you your attorney about all of past injuries, even from your childhood. The insurance company will work very hard to try to connect previous injuries, even from way back in your childhood, to your current condition. The important issue is that your medical records show that you recovered from each of your previous injuries or at least improved to a certain point.

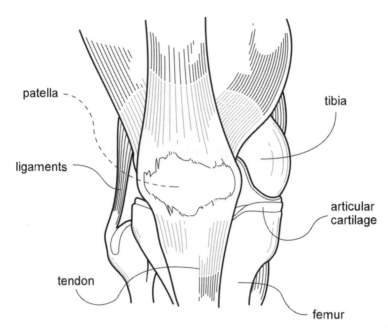

patella

ligaments

tendon

tibia

articular cartilage

femur

For example, if you had a high school football injury to your knee and now you are claiming that your knee was injured in your golf cart accident, they will claim that treatment you are getting now is really from your football injury and not your current accident. In other words, they will make you out to be a faker or even a liar.

We must carefully document all of your past injuries and your recovery from them to distinguish your new injuries and conditions. The insurance for the responsible party is liable for your damages caused by the accident, and you need your attorney to properly present the evidence to best advance your case.

Chapter Eleven

Damages

Your damages may consist of monetary and nonmonetary losses. Lost income, medical bills, loss of consortium, future medical bills, pain and suffering, and loss of enjoyment of life are some of the damages that follow an accident. Recovering the losses from an accident is the goal of personal injury lawsuits. The injured party, also known as the plaintiff, seeks to be put back in the place where he or she would have been had the accident never occurred. This requires evidence to be presented by the plaintiff proving the damages he or she suffered.

What is the amount of money the plaintiff should demand? This answer varies on a case-by-case basis. Personal injury cases may allow economic damages such as medical bills, lost support and services, value of the damaged personal property, loss of consortium, loss wages, and any other economic loss that would not have occurred except for the injury giving rise to the cause of action.[35]

a. Loss of Consortium

What has changed between you and partner since the accident? Think about it. Has your partner's mood or personality changed? Was there a change in household chores? Are your movie nights cancelled because your partner is in a wheelchair and does not want to leave the house? Did your traveling come to a stop? These are a few examples of the questions you must consider. Ask yourself what has changed, and even if it is something small, do not hesitate to inform your attorney of this change.

You are not the only person in a relationship who has suffered because of a partner's injury. Many people face loss of intimacy and depression, which can even lead to seeking psychological treatment and marriage counseling. I recommend you use a journal to note the marital issues that have occurred since the accident. Keep in mind the defendant may seek this evidence during discovery, so you should notate on the front page "for my attorney only."

b. Medical Treatment and Bills

The most important advice I can give you about medical bills is to keep a list of the providers where you receive treatment. If you forget to mention a doctor, the amount of your damages may not be accurate, and you could potentially receive less from the defendant than you need to recover. Moreover, if there is information that your attorney or court does not receive from you and the other side presents it, then your case could be adversely affected.

During your treatment process, listen to your physician and attend your appointments. The treatment plan is more effective when you follow the advice of your doctor. The patients who skip their appointments may also have to face questions from the defendant. It may appear that you are not as injured as you claim when you skip doctor's appointments. Always remember that the defendant does not want to pay you; therefore, do not give the defendant reasons to dispute your injuries and not pay you what you are properly and legally owed.

As previously mentioned, it is very important that you maintain a list of providers you have seen to provide accurate damages to your attorney and the court. In addition, record your mileage to and from the physician appointments. The medicals bills will be calculated and sent to the defendant during the discovery process. You or your attorney should continue to request updated medical records and bills throughout the treatment process to ensure the file is up to date and accurate.

c. Punitive Damages

In some cases, the injured may seek punitive damages when the harm caused was a result of the defendant's gross negligence. However, there is a cap in Florida limiting the amount of punitive damages available to recover unless the defendant was intoxicated. Punitive damages are limited to three times the amount of compensatory or economic damages awarded to each claimant or the sum of $500,000. [36] In regard to intoxication, it is defined as a blood or breath alcohol level of 0.08 percent or higher.[37]

Keep in mind that the defendant may request information pertaining to your drinking habits during the discovery process. This is usually to determine whether you were intoxicated at the time of the accident and whether you have any other substance abuse problems.

d. Loss Wages

To calculate your loss wages, start by calculating the days you were unable to work as a result of the accident from the date it occurred to present. It is best to keep a notebook where you can record the days you were scheduled to work and were unable to because of injuries, medical appointments, or other issues pertaining to your losses.

e. Future Losses

Consider both present damages and future losses. The injuries that you sustained in the present may worsen or prevent you from ever working again. On the other hand, you may never feel pain once your treatment ends and go on living your life as you did prior to the accident. Either way the possibility of long-term damage must be considered for the best interest of you and your family.

Please understand future damages are often difficult to calculate, which is why I suggest that the injured party obtain a permanency rating from the physician who treated the injuries. The permanency rating will allow the defendant and court to see the extent of the injuries and the possibility of recovery, if there is any possibility. Many attorneys use their knowledge in personal injury cases along with the doctor's final report to determine an amount to demand from the defendant.

Chapter Twelve

The Process

a. Medical treatment

The first priority after handling the scene of the accident is to get proper medical treatment. You should go to the hospital or emergency care clinic within twenty-four hours of the crash and the sooner, the better. You may not feel like you have major injuries, but often the symptoms of your injuries won't show up for several days. That is why you need the doctor run tests to properly diagnose you.

You will be more bruised and have more pain one or two days after the crash, but do not wait until then to get checked out. Most emergency room treatment facilities will treat you regardless of your ability to pay. After that, you will need a payment source for your medical treatment in most cases.

If your doctor requires further treatment after your initial examination, follow his or her instructions. Do not neglect your health. There are also times when you may be recommended to another doctor after you have reached your maximum medical improvement (MMI), which means the current doctor has improved your condition as much as possible. You may later need injections, surgery, or another type of therapy if you cannot manage the pain. Your attorney should request a permanency rating from the physician to evaluate the extent of the injuries and the possibility of recovery.

b. Demand

A demand is generally sent to the defendant after the attorney reviews the injuries suffered by the plaintiff. This is done by reviewing medical records. I use my knowledge in personal injury and the insurance field along with the doctor's final report to determine an amount to demand from the defendant. Keep in mind, as previously mentioned, the defendant will almost always counter a demand and argue the injuries are not permanent. Do not be discouraged by the defendant denying your demand and initially offering a lesser amount. This is part of the process.

If the insurance company is being unreasonable, your attorney will likely gather more evidence of your damages by obtaining a report from an expert. Newer automobiles have a black box in the car, and there are times when the parties may request an expert to pull the data from the black box. There are experts in various areas to assist with specific reports that we may later use at trial.

c. File Suit

The next step after the insurance company denies your demand is filing suit. If the insurance company does not agree to settle based on the demand sent, then a suit is filed, and the parties involved are served. A complaint naming the parties and allegations against them is filed with the court, and the defendants are served by a process server. After the lawsuit is filed in the court and the parties are served, the discovery process begins.

d. Discovery

The discovery process will consist of several documents requesting information. You will likely be served with Request for Admissions, Interrogatories, and a Request to Produce. Each of these discovery items have deadlines and must be responded to completely and accurately. I recommend working with your attorney and the firm in answering these questions to avoid errors. A simple mistake in answering your questions or providing documents can negatively impact your case.

In addition, to the documents and questions that will be served upon you, the insurance company will likely request a Compulsory Medical Examination (CME) to take place at a specified time and date. The CME is when a doctor, one the insurance company selects, does an exam and provides the report to the insurance company. Many clients ask me if this sort of exam is permitted by the insurance company. The answer is yes because the Florida Rules of Civil Procedure allow the defendant to have their doctor examine you. Remember, you are suing them, and they are attempting to challenge your injuries. It is best to have your attorney present at this examination. I usually attend my clients' exams and have a court reporter present and request copies of the medical report prepared by the insurance company's doctor.

e. Depositions

The insurance company is going to ask you questions similar to those previously asked in your Interrogatories. The question regarding the circumstances surrounding the accident seems to appear often. This is where you will be asked questions to determine what you did to avoid the accident or what you saw prior to the accident. It is important that you pay attention to your surroundings when you are on the road because if you inform the insurance company/adverse party that you did not and somehow acted negligently, then a portion of fault may be placed on you.

There will be questions about your hobbies and activities that you did prior to the accident. You will be asked about your employment and loss of wages. There will be inquiries into your personal life. The best way to prepare for the depositions is to take notes of the difficulty, pain, and all other details that may refresh your memory prior to the depositions. Many people have difficulty remembering things and notating pain, missed days of work, cancelled trips resulting from injuries, and so forth. Documenting this information will help you remember the same on the day of your deposition and for your trial testimony.

f. Mediation

Florida courts require the parties attend mediation prior to trial. There is no requirement that you settle, but you must attend mediation. The goal here is to obtain the best settlement for you, and if the insurance company does not agree to an amount that would make you whole again, then we can continue to pursue the lawsuit and litigate the matter in court.

g. Trial

When a case proceeds to trial, the court will set the trial date, and the parties will begin asking the court for evidence to be admitted or excluded. The Florida rules of evidence and civil procedure will apply during this entire process. At the time of trial, the parties and witnesses will be able to explain and present their side to the judge, and if there is a jury, then the jury as well. The judge will decide which evidence can be heard while the jury determines the weight of the evidence presented.

Preparing your testimony before trial is mandatory, in my opinion. It is good to have a mock trial to make you comfortable with the possible questions that will arise during the real trial. In my previous cases, I have asked my clients to participate in mock trials and later asked the mock jury their individual opinions. This helps us in every aspect of the trial from opening statements to closing arguments.

h. Appeal

A case may get dismissed prior to trial or proceed to trial and have an unfavorable verdict. In some of these instances where the attorney and you find there is sufficient evidence to find in your favor, an appeal may be filed. In addition, an insurance company will often appeal a verdict with the hopes of overturning the judgment or at least delaying payment that they owe you.

Chapter Thirteen

Post-Settlement or Verdict

After the settlement or verdict, the medical and insurance liens must be paid before the attorney can disburse the proceeds to the injured client. A lien is a security on real or personal property for the payment of the debt owed to the creditor.[38] Accident attorneys have agreements with many medical providers to work on what is called a Letter of Protection. This Letter of Protection is an agreement that the attorney will pay the medical facility after a settlement or judgment is paid in your case. This relieves the crash victim of having to worry about the financial pressure of how to pay for the necessary medical care.

Many attorneys will negotiate with the lien creditors upon settlement to reduce the amount you owe. This is a process I always do to provide my client with the best possible recovery of damages. The same concept applies to funds paid by insurance companies and Medicaid/Medicare. Your health insurance or Medicare/Medicaid may cover your hospital bills; however, they will attach to your claim to later be reimbursed once you settle or there is a final judgment.[39] The reimbursement will be for a portion of the funds paid for medical services rendered from the accident.

Although most parties consent to receiving treatment after an accident, there are some who are admitted in an emergency situation and unable to consent. Even in such instances, there is an implied consent, and parties are still liable for the services rendered.[40] As a result, many injured plaintiffs will have hospital liens that must be satisfied.

Unlike most liens, hospital liens do not attach to property; rather, it attaches to the proceeds of a final judgment or case settlement pertaining to the accident that caused the injuries treated by the hospital.[41] The hospital does not need to bring suit, as the hospital lien would attach only after the injured has brought suit. In addition to the hospital's lien, the physician may also impose a lien to ensure compensation for their services.[42]

Notes

1   *See* DMV.org
2   *Nucci v. Target Corp.*, 162 So. 3d 146, 153 (Fla. 4th DCA 2015).
3   *See Id.*
4   *See Id.*
5   Fla. Stat. § 316.650.
6   *Birge v. Charron,* 107 So. 3d 350, 353 (Fla. 2012).
7   *Servello & Sons, Inc. v. Sims,* 922 So. 2d 234 (Fla. 5th DCA 2005).
8   *Id.*
9   *Id.*
10 *Id.*
11 *Birge v. Charron,* 107 So. 3d 350, 353 (Fla. 2012).
12 § 316.066 (5)
13 *Sottilaro v. Figueroa,* 86 So. 3d 505 (Fla. 2d DCA 2012).
14 *Birge v. Charron,* 107 So. 3d 350, 353 (Fla. 2012)
15 *Id.*
16 Pre-trial Settlement Percentage: Statistics on Personal Injury Settlements, THE LAW DICTIONARY,https://thelawdictionary.org/article/pre-trial-settlement-percentage-statistics-on-personal-injury-settlements/ (last visited Jan. 12, 2019).
17 Motorcycle Insurance Minimum Requirements in Florida, DEPARTMENT OF MOTOR VEHICLE, https://www.dmv.org/fl-florida/insurance/motorcycle-insurance-minimum-requirements.php (last visited Jan. 12, 2019).

18 *Id.*

19 *Id.*

20 Kevin Spear, *Bicycling fatalities are up nationally; Florida struggles to improve safety,* August 23, 2017, ORLANDO SENTINEL, https://www.orlandosentinel.com/news/os-bike-study-national-fatalities-20170823-story.html.

21 Douglas Ray, *Study of bicycle crashes in Florida finds clusters of danger,* July 4, 2017, THE GAINESVILLE SUN, https://www.gainesville.com/news/20170704/study-of-bicycle-crashes-in-florida-finds-clusters-of-danger.

22 Vehicle Insurance Questions and Answers, FLORIDA DEPARTMENT OF TRANSPORTATION, https://www.flhsmv.gov/ddl/frfaqgen.html (last visited Jan. 11, 2019).

23 Fla. Stat. § 626.9541.

24 Fla. Stat. § 627.736.

25 *Id.*

26 *Id.*

27 *See* Fla. Stat. § 768.81.

28 *Id.*

29 *Lenhart v. Basora,* 100 So. 3d 1177, 1178 (Fla. 4th DCA 2012).

30 *Id.*

31 *Id.* at 1179.

32 *Antico v. Sindt Trucking, Inc.,* 148 So. 3d 163 (Fla. 1st DCA 2014).

33 *Id.*

34 *Id.*

35 Fla. Stat. § 768.81.

36 Fla. Stat. § 768.73.

37 *See* § 15:19. Actions in which the defendant was intoxicated, 6 Fla. Prac., Personal Injury & Wrongful Death Actions § 15:19 (2018–2019 ed.).

38 *See* Meta Calder, *Florida's Hospital Lien Laws,* 21 Fla. St. U.L. Rev. 341, 342–45 (1993).

39 *Id.* at 368.

40 *See Id.* at 342–45.

41 *Id.*

42 *See* 39 A.L.R.5th 787 (Originally published in 1996).

Appendix I

MODEL INSTRUCTION NO. 1

Automobile collision; comparative negligence; single claimant and defendant; no counterclaim; no-fault issue; witnesses testifying in foreign language; instructions for beginning and end of case; use of special verdict in burden of proof and damage instructions

Facts of the hypothetical case:

John Doe was injured when the automobile he was driving collided with one driven by Rachel Rowe. John Doe sued Rachel Rowe. Rachel Rowe pleaded comparative negligence. Questions of negligence, comparative negligence, causation, permanency of John Doe's injuries and damages are to be submitted to the jury. Traffic Accident Reconstruction experts testified in the case. There is no *Fabre* issue. Several witnesses will testify in Spanish.

The court's instruction:

These instructions illustrate: (1) instructions to be given at the beginning of the case, (2) instructions to be given before final argument and the closing instructions to be given after final argument. Instruction number (2), to be given before final argument, also illustrates how the court could utilize the Special Verdict questions in the burden of proof portion of the instruction.

(1) Instruction for the beginning of the case:

[101.2] *Members of the jury*, do you solemnly swear or affirm that you will well and truly try this case between John Doe and Rachel Rowe, and a true verdict render according to the law and evidence?

[202.1] You have now taken an oath to serve as jurors in this trial. Before we begin, I am going to tell you about the rules of law that apply to this case. It is my intention to give you [all] [most] of the rules of law but it might be that I will not know for sure all of the law that might apply in this case until all of the evidence is presented. However, I can anticipate most of the law and give it to you at the beginning of the trial so that you can better understand what to be looking for as the evidence is presented. If I later decide that different law applies to the case, I will call that to your attention. In any event, at the end of the evidence I will give you the final instructions that you must use to decide this case and it is those instructions on which you must base your verdict. At that time, you will have a complete written set of the instructions so you do not have to memorize what I am about to tell you.

[401.2] The claims and defenses in this case are as follows. John Doe claims that Rachel Rowe was negligent in the operation of the vehicle she was driving which caused him harm.

Rachel Rowe denies that claim and also claims that John Doe was himself negligent in the operation of his vehicle, which caused his harm.

The parties must prove their claims by the greater weight of the evidence. I will now define some of the terms you will use in deciding this case.

[401.3] "Greater weight of the evidence" means the more persuasive and convincing force and effect of the entire *evidence* in the case.

[401.4] Negligence is the failure to use reasonable care, which is the care that a reasonably careful person would use under like circumstances. Negligence is doing something that a reasonably careful person would not do under like circumstances or failing to do something that a reasonably careful person would do under like circumstances.

If there is an issue about the applicability of a statute
this instruction would be omitted at this time.

[401.9] *(Read or paraphrase the applicable statute or refer to the ordinance or regulation admitted in evidence.)* Violation of this statute is evidence of negligence. It is not, however, conclusive evidence of negligence. If you find that Rachel Rowe violated this statute, you may consider that fact, together with the other facts and circumstances, in deciding whether *she* was negligent.

[401.12(a)] Negligence is a legal cause of loss, injury, or damage if it directly and in natural and continuous sequence produces or contributes substantially to producing such loss, injury, or damage, so that it can reasonably be said that, but for the negligence, the loss, injury, or damage would not have occurred.

[401.12(b)] In order to be regarded as a legal cause of loss, injury, or damage negligence need not be the only cause. Negligence may be a legal cause of loss, injury, or damage even though it operates in combination with some other cause if the negligence contributes substantially to producing such loss, injury, or damage.

-2-

[401.18] The issues you must decide on John Doe's claim against Rachel Rowe are whether Rachel Rowe was negligent in the operation of her vehicle, and, if so, whether that negligence was a legal cause of the loss, injury, or damage to John Doe.

[401.21] If the greater weight of the evidence does not support John Doe's claim, your verdict should be for Rachel Rowe.

[401.22] If, however, the greater weight of the evidence supports John Doe's claim, then you shall consider the defense raised by Rachel Rowe.

[401.22(a)] On *that* defense, the issue for you to decide is whether John Doe was himself negligent in the operation of his vehicle and, if so, whether that negligence was a contributing legal cause of injury or damage to John Doe.

[401.23] If the greater weight of the evidence does not support Rachel Rowe's defense and the greater weight of the evidence supports John Doe's claim, then your verdict should be for John Doe in the total amount of his damages.

If, however, the greater weight of the evidence shows that both John Doe and Rachel Rowe were negligent and that the negligence of each contributed as a legal cause of loss, injury, or damage sustained by John Doe, you should decide and write on the verdict form, *which I will give you at the end of the case,* what percentage of the total negligence of both parties to this action was caused by each of them.

[501.3] If your verdict is for Rachel Rowe, you will not consider the matter of damages. But, if the greater weight of the evidence supports John Doe's claim, you should determine and write on the verdict form, in dollars, the total amount of money that the greater weight of the evidence shows will fairly and adequately compensate John Doe for the following elements of damage to the extent that they have not been paid and are not payable by personal injury protection benefits, including damage that John Doe is reasonably certain to incur in the future:

The reasonable expense of hospitalization and medical care and treatment necessarily or reasonably obtained by John Doe in the past, or to be so obtained in the future.

- 3 -

Any earnings lost in the past, and any loss of ability to earn money in the future.

You must next decide whether John Doe's injury, resulting from the incident in this case, is permanent. An injury is permanent if it, in whole or in part, consists of an injury that the evidence shows is permanent to a reasonable degree of medical probability.

If the greater weight of the evidence does not establish that John Doe's injury is permanent, then your verdict is complete. If, however, the greater weight of the evidence shows that John Doe's injury is permanent, you should also award damages for this additional element of damage:

Any bodily injury sustained by John Doe and any resulting pain and suffering, disability or physical impairment, disfigurement, mental anguish, inconvenience or loss of capacity for the enjoyment of life experienced in the past, or to be experienced in the future. There is no exact standard for measuring such damage. The amount should be fair and just, in the light of the evidence.

[501.5] In determining the total amount of damages, you should not make any reduction because of the negligence, if any, of John Doe. The court will enter a judgment based on your verdict and, if you find that John Doe was negligent in any degree, the court, in entering judgment, will reduce the total amount of damages by the percentage of negligence, which you find was caused by John Doe.

[501.6] If the greater weight of the evidence shows that John Doe has been permanently injured, you may consider his life expectancy. Mortality tables *may be* received in evidence and, if they are, you may consider *them* in determining how long John Doe may be expected to live. Mortality tables are not binding on you, but may be considered together with other evidence in the case bearing on John Doe's health, age and physical condition, before and after the injury, in determining the probable length of his life.

[501.7] Any amount of damages, which you allow for future medical expenses or loss of ability to earn money in the future, should be reduced to its present money value, and only the present money value of these future economic damages should be included in your verdict. The present money value of future economic damages is the sum of money needed now which, together with what that sum will earn in the future, will compensate John Doe for these losses as they are actually experienced in future years.

- 4 -

[601.1] In deciding this case, it is your duty as jurors to decide the issues, and only those issues, that I submit for your determination *at the end of the case* and to answer certain questions I *will* ask you to answer on a special form, called a special verdict. You must come to an agreement about what your answers will be. Your agreed-upon answers to my questions are called your jury verdict.

In reaching your verdict, you must think about and weigh the testimony and any documents, photographs, or other material that has been received in evidence. You may also consider any facts that were admitted or agreed to by the lawyers. Your job is to determine what the facts are. You may use reason and common sense to reach conclusions. You may draw reasonable inferences from the evidence. But you should not guess about things that were not covered here. And, you must always apply the law as I *finally* explain it to you *at the end of the case*.

[601.2(a)] Let me speak briefly about witnesses. In evaluating the believability of any witness and the weight you will give the testimony of any witness, you may properly consider the demeanor of the witness while testifying; the frankness or lack of frankness of the witness; the intelligence of the witness; any interest the witness may have in the outcome of the case; the means and opportunity the witness had to know the facts about which the witness testified; the ability of the witness to remember the matters about which the witness testified; and the reasonableness of the testimony of the witness, considered in the light of all the evidence in the case and in the light of your own experience and common sense.

[601.2(b)] Some of the testimony *you hear may be* in the form of opinions about certain technical subjects.

You may accept such opinion testimony, reject it, or give it the weight you think it deserves, considering the knowledge, skill, experience, training, or education of the witness, the reasons given by the witness for the opinion expressed, and all the other evidence in the case.

[202.2] Now that you have heard the law, I want to let you know what you can expect as the trial proceeds.

Opening Statements: **In a few moments, the attorneys will each have a chance to make what are called opening statements. In an opening statement, an attorney is allowed to give you [his] [her] views about what the evidence will be in the trial and what you are likely to see and hear in the testimony.**

Evidentiary Phase: **After the attorneys' opening statements the plaintiff will bring his witnesses and evidence to you, followed by the defendant.**

Evidence: **Evidence is the information that the law allows you to see or hear in deciding this case. Evidence includes the testimony of the witnesses, documents, and anything else that I instruct you to consider.**

Witnesses: **A witness is a person who takes an oath to tell the truth and then answers attorneys' questions for the jury. The answering of attorneys' questions by witnesses is called "giving testimony." Testimony means statements that are made when someone has sworn an oath to tell the truth.**

The plaintiff's lawyer will normally ask a witness the questions first. That is called direct examination. Then the defense lawyer may ask the same witness additional questions about whatever the witness has testified to. That is called cross-examination. Certain documents or other evidence may also be shown to you during direct or cross-examination. After the plaintiff's witnesses have testified, the defendant will have the opportunity to put witnesses on the stand and go through the same process. Then the plaintiff's lawyer gets to do cross-examination. The process is designed to be fair to both sides.

It is important that you remember that testimony comes from witnesses. The attorneys do not give testimony and they are not themselves witnesses.

Objections: **Sometimes the attorneys will disagree about the rules for trial procedure when a question is asked of a witness. When that happens, one of the lawyers may make what is called an "objection." The rules for a trial can be complicated, and there are many reasons for the attorneys to object. You should simply wait for me to decide how to proceed. If I say that an objection is "sustained," that means you should disregard the question and the witness may not answer the question. If I say that the objection is "overruled," that means the witness may answer the question.**

When there is an objection and I make a decision, you must not assume from that decision that I have any particular opinion other than that the rules for conducting a trial are being correctly followed. If I say a question may not

- 6 -

be asked or answered, you must not try to guess what the answer would have been. That is against the rules, too.

Side Bar Conferences: **Sometimes I will need to speak to the attorneys about legal elements of the case that are not appropriate for the jury to hear. The attorneys and I will try to have as few of these conferences as possible while you are giving us your valuable time in the courtroom. But, if we do have to have such a conference during testimony, we will try to hold the conference at the side of my desk so that we do not have to take a break and ask you to leave the courtroom.**

Recesses: **Breaks in an ongoing trial are usually called "recesses." During a recess you still have your duties as a juror and must follow the rules, even while having coffee, at lunch, or at home.**

Instructions Before Closing Arguments: **After all the evidence has been presented to you, I will** *again* **instruct you on the law that you must follow. At that time you will have a written set of the instructions for your use.**

Closing Arguments: **The attorneys will then have the opportunity to make their final presentations to you, which are called closing arguments.**

Final Instructions: **After you have heard the closing arguments, I will instruct you further in the law as well as explain to you the procedures you must follow to decide the case.**

Deliberations: **After you hear the final jury instructions, you will go to the jury room and discuss and decide the questions I have put on your verdict form. [You will have a copy of the jury instructions to use during your discussions.] The discussions you have and the decisions you make are usually called "jury deliberations." Your deliberations are absolutely private and neither I nor anyone else will be with you in the jury room.**

Verdict: **When you have finished answering the questions, you will give the verdict form to the bailiff, and we will all return to the courtroom where your verdict will be read. When that is completed, you will be released from your assignment as a juror.**

What are the rules?

Finally, before we begin the trial, I want to give you just a brief explanation of rules you must follow as the case proceeds.

Keeping an Open Mind. **You must pay close attention to the testimony and other evidence as it comes into the trial. However, you must avoid forming any final opinion or telling anyone else your views on the case until you begin your deliberations. This rule requires you to keep an open mind until you have heard all of the evidence and is designed to prevent you from influencing how your fellow jurors think until they have heard all of the evidence and had an opportunity to form their own opinions. The time and place for coming to your final opinions and speaking about them with your fellow jurors is during deliberations in the jury room, after all of the evidence has been presented, closing arguments have been made, and I have instructed you on the law. It is important that you hear all of the facts and that you hear the law and how to apply it before you start deciding anything.**

Consider Only the Evidence. **It is the things you hear and see in this courtroom that matter in this trial. The law tells us that a juror can consider only the testimony and other evidence that all the other jurors have also heard and seen in the presence of the judge and the lawyers. Doing anything else is wrong and is against the law. That means that you cannot do any work or investigation of your own about the case. You cannot obtain on your own any information about the case or about anyone involved in the case, from any source whatsoever, including the Internet, and you cannot visit places mentioned in the trial.**

Do not provide any information about this case to anyone, including friends or family members. Do not let anyone, including the closest family members, make comments to you or ask questions about the trial. Similarly, it is important that you avoid reading any newspaper accounts or watching or listening to television or radio comments that have anything to do with this case or its subject.

No Mid-Trial Discussions. **When we are in a recess, do not discuss anything about the trial or the case with each other or with anyone else. If attorneys approach you, don't speak with them. The law says they are to avoid contact with you. If an attorney will not look at you or speak to you, do not be offended or form a conclusion about that behavior. The attorney is not supposed to interact with jurors outside of the courtroom and is only following the rules. The attorney is not being impolite. If an attorney or anyone else does try to speak with you or says something about the case in your presence, please inform the bailiff immediately.**

Only the Jury Decides. **Only you get to deliberate and answer the verdict questions at the end of the trial. I will not intrude into your deliberations at all. I am required to be neutral. You should not assume that I prefer one decision over another. You should not try to guess what my opinion is about any part of the case. It would be wrong for you to conclude that anything I say or do means that I am for one side or another in the trial. Discussing and deciding the facts is your job alone.**

[202.3] If you would like to take notes during the trial, you may do so. On the other hand, of course, you are not required to take notes if you do not want to. That will be left up to you individually.

You will be provided with a note pad and a pen for use if you wish to take notes. Any notes that you take will be for your personal use. However, you should not take them with you from the courtroom. During recesses, the bailiff will take possession of your notes and will return them to you when we reconvene. After you have completed your deliberations, the bailiff will deliver your notes to me. They will be destroyed. No one will ever read your notes.

If you take notes, do not get so involved in note-taking that you become distracted from the proceedings. Your notes should be used only as aids to your memory.

Whether or not you take notes, you should rely on your memory of the evidence and you should not be unduly influenced by the notes of other jurors. Notes are not entitled to any greater weight than each juror's memory of the evidence.

[202.4] During the trial, you may have a question you think should be asked of a witness. If so, there is a procedure by which you may request that I ask the witness a question. After all the attorneys have completed their questioning of the witness, you should raise your hand if you have a question. I will then give you sufficient time to write the question on a piece of paper, fold it, and give it to the bailiff, who will pass it to me. You must not show your question to anyone or discuss it with anyone.

I will then review the question with the attorneys. Under our law, only certain evidence may be considered by a jury in determining a verdict. You are bound by the same rules of evidence that control the attorneys' questions. If I decide that the question may not be asked under our rules of evidence, I

- 9 -

will tell you. Otherwise, I will direct the question to the witness. The attorneys may then ask follow-up questions if they wish. If there are additional questions from jurors, we will follow the same procedure again.

By providing this procedure, I do not mean to suggest that you must or should submit written questions for witnesses. In most cases, the lawyers will have asked the necessary questions.

[202.5] *During the trial,* some witnesses may testify in Spanish which will be interpreted in English.

The evidence you are to consider is only that provided through the official court interpreters. Although some of you may know Spanish, it is important that all jurors consider the same evidence. Therefore, you must accept the English interpretation. You must disregard any different meaning.

If, however, during the testimony there is a question as to the accuracy of the English interpretation, you should bring this matter to my attention immediately by raising your hand. You should not ask your question or make any comment about the interpretation in the presence of the other jurors, or otherwise share your question or concern with any of them. I will take steps to see if your question can be answered and any discrepancy resolved. If, however, after such efforts a discrepancy remains, I emphasize that you must rely only upon the official English interpretation as provided by the court interpreter and disregard any other contrary interpretation.

The attorneys will now present their opening statements after which you will begin hearing the evidence.

(2) Instruction before final argument:

[401.1] Members of the jury, you have now heard and received all of the evidence in this case. I am now going to tell you about the rules of law that you must use in reaching your verdict. You will recall at the beginning of the case I told you that if, at the end of the case I decided that different law applies, I would tell you so. These instructions are, *however, the same as* [if different explain how] what I gave you at the beginning and it is these rules of law that you must now follow. When I finish telling you about the rules of law, the attorneys will present their final arguments and you will then retire to decide your verdict.

[401.2] The claims and defenses in this case are as follows. John Doe claims that Rachel Rowe was negligent in the operation of the vehicle she was driving which caused him harm.

Rachel Rowe denies that claim and also claims that John Doe was himself negligent in the operation of his vehicle, which caused his harm.

The parties must prove their claims by the greater weight of the evidence. I will now define some of the terms you will use in deciding this case.

[401.3] "Greater weight of the evidence" means the more persuasive and convincing force and effect of the entire evidence in the case.

[401.4] Negligence is the failure to use reasonable care, which is the care that a reasonably careful person would use under like circumstances. Negligence is doing something that a reasonably careful person would not do under like circumstances or failing to do something that a reasonably careful person would do under like circumstances.

[401.9] *(Read or paraphrase the applicable statute or refer to the ordinance or regulation admitted in evidence.)* Violation of this statute is evidence of negligence. It is not, however, conclusive evidence of negligence. If you find that Rachel Rowe violated this statute, you may consider that fact, together with the other facts and circumstances, in deciding whether *she* was negligent.

[401.12(a)] Negligence is a legal cause of loss, injury, or damage if it directly and in natural and continuous sequence produces or contributes substantially to producing such loss, injury, or damage, so that it can reasonably be said that, but for the negligence, the loss, injury, or damage would not have occurred.

[401.12(b)] In order to be regarded as a legal cause of loss, injury, or damage negligence need not be the only cause. Negligence may be a legal cause of loss, injury, or damage even though it operates in combination with some other cause if the negligence contributes substantially to producing such loss, injury, or damage.

[401.18] The issues you must decide on John Doe's claim against Rachel Rowe are whether Rachel Rowe was negligent in the operation of her vehicle, and, if so, whether that negligence was a legal cause of the loss, injury, or damage to John Doe.

You will be given a Special Verdict to use in this case. The first question in the Special Verdict is:

1. Was there negligence on the part of Defendant, RACHEL ROWE, which was a legal cause of damage to Plaintiff, JOHN DOE?

YES _____   NO _____

[401.21, 22] *If the greater weight of the evidence supports John Doe's claim, you will answer that question "YES." If, however, your answer to question 1 is "NO," your verdict is for the Defendant, and you should not proceed further, except to date and sign the Special Verdict and return it to the courtroom.*

If *you answered the first question YES*, then you shall consider the defense raised by Rachel Rowe.

[401.22(a)] On *that* defense, the issue for you to decide is whether John Doe was himself negligent in the operation of his vehicle and, if so, whether that negligence was a contributing legal cause of injury or damage to John Doe. *In connection with that defense, the second question in the Special Verdict is:*

2. Was there negligence on the part of Plaintiff, JOHN DOE, which was a legal cause of his damage?

YES _____   NO _____

[401.23] *If the greater weight of the evidence supports Rachel Rowe's defense, you will answer that question "Yes." If, however, your answer to that question is "NO" and the greater weight of the evidence supports John Doe's claim, then your verdict should be for John Doe in the total amount of his damages and you will skip the third question in the Special Verdict and proceed directly to the questions concerning damages.*

If, however, the greater weight of the evidence shows that both John Doe and Rachel Rowe were negligent and that the negligence of each contributed as a legal cause of loss, injury, or damage sustained by John Doe, you should decide and write on the verdict form what percentage of the total negligence of both parties to this action was caused by each of them. *In that connection, the third question in the Special Verdict is:*

- 12 -

3. State the percentage of negligence which was a legal cause of damage to Plaintiff, JOHN DOE, that you charge to:

RACHEL ROWE _____%

JOHN DOE _____%

[501.3] If your verdict is for Rachel Rowe, you will not consider the matter of damages. But, if the greater weight of the evidence supports John Doe's claim *and you answered the first question "YES,"* you should determine and write on the verdict form, in dollars, the total amount of money that the greater weight of the evidence shows will fairly and adequately compensate John Doe for the following elements of damage to the extent that they have not been paid and are not payable by personal injury protection benefits, including damage that John Doe is reasonably certain to incur in the future:

The reasonable expense of hospitalization and medical care and treatment necessarily or reasonably obtained by John Doe in the past, or to be so obtained in the future:

Any earnings lost in the past, and any loss of ability to earn money in the future.

These appear as questions 4 and 5 in the Special Verdict.

You must next decide whether John Doe's injury, resulting from the incident in this case, is permanent. An injury is permanent if it, in whole or in part, consists of an injury that the evidence shows is permanent to a reasonable degree of medical probability.

If the greater weight of the evidence does not establish that John Doe's injury is permanent, then your verdict is complete. If, however, the greater weight of the evidence shows that John Doe's injury is permanent, you should also award damages for this additional element of damage:

Any bodily injury sustained by John Doe and any resulting pain and suffering, disability or physical impairment, disfigurement, mental anguish, inconvenience or loss of capacity for the enjoyment of life experienced in the past, or to be experienced in the future. There is no exact standard for

- 13 -

measuring such damage. The amount should be fair and just, in the light of the evidence.

This appears as question 6 in the Special Verdict.

[501.4] In determining the total amount of damages, you should not make any reduction because of the negligence, if any, of John Doe. The court will enter a judgment based on your verdict and, if you find that John Doe was negligent in any degree, the court, in entering judgment, will reduce the total amount of damages by the percentage of negligence which you find was caused by John Doe.

[501.6] If the greater weight of the evidence shows that John Doe has been permanently injured, you may consider his life expectancy. The mortality tables received in evidence may be considered in determining how long John Doe may be expected to live. Mortality tables are not binding on you, but may be considered together with other evidence in the case bearing on John Doe's health, age and physical condition, before and after the injury, in determining the probable length of his life.

[501.7] Any amount of damages which you allow for future medical expenses or loss of ability to earn money in the future should be reduced to its present money value, and only the present money value of these future economic damages should be included in your verdict. The present money value of future economic damages is the sum of money needed now which, together with what that sum will earn in the future, will compensate John Doe for these losses as they are actually experienced in future years.

[601.1] In deciding this case, it is your duty as jurors to decide the issues, and only those issues, that I submit for your determination and to answer the questions I *have asked* you to answer on the special verdict. You must come to an agreement about what your answers will be. Your agreed-upon answers to my questions are called your jury verdict.

In reaching your verdict, you must think about and weigh the testimony and any documents, photographs, or other material that has been received in evidence. You may also consider any facts that were admitted or agreed to by the lawyers. Your job is to determine what the facts are. You may use reason and common sense to reach conclusions. You may draw reasonable inferences from the evidence. But you should not guess about things that were not covered here. And, you must always apply the law as I have explained it to you.

[601.2(a)] Let me speak briefly about witnesses. In evaluating the believability of any witness and the weight you will give the testimony of any witness, you may properly consider the demeanor of the witness while testifying; the frankness or lack of frankness of the witness; the intelligence of the witness; any interest the witness may have in the outcome of the case; the means and opportunity the witness had to know the facts about which the witness testified; the ability of the witness to remember the matters about which the witness testified; and the reasonableness of the testimony of the witness, considered in the light of all the evidence in the case and in the light of your own experience and common sense.

[601.2(b)] Some of the testimony before you was in the form of opinions about certain technical subjects.

You may accept such opinion testimony, reject it, or give it the weight you think it deserves, considering the knowledge, skill, experience, training, or education of the witness, the reasons given by the witness for the opinion expressed, and all the other evidence in the case.

[601.3] Some witnesses testified in Spanish during this trial, which had to be interpreted into English. The evidence you are to consider is only that provided through the official court interpreters. Although some of you may know Spanish, it is important that all jurors consider the same evidence. Therefore, you must base your decision on the evidence presented in the English interpretation. You must disregard any different meaning.

[601.5] That is the law you must follow in deciding this case. The attorneys for the parties will now present their final arguments. When they are through, I will have a few final instructions about your deliberations.

(3) Instruction following closing arguments:

[700] Members of the jury, you have now heard all the evidence, my instructions on the law that you must apply in reaching your verdict, and the closing arguments of the attorneys. You will shortly retire to the jury room to decide this case. Before you do so, I have a few last instructions for you.

- 15 -

You will have in the jury room all of the evidence that was received during the trial. In reaching your decision, do not do any research on your own or as a group. Do not use dictionaries, the Internet, or other reference materials. Do not investigate the case or conduct any experiments. Do not contact anyone to assist you, such as a family accountant, doctor, or lawyer. Do not visit or view the scene of any event involved in this case. If you happen to pass by the scene, do not stop or investigate. All jurors must see or hear the same evidence at the same time. Do not read, listen to, or watch any news accounts of this trial.

Any notes you have taken during the trial may be taken to the jury room for use during your discussions. Your notes are simply an aid to your own memory, and neither your notes nor those of any other juror are binding or conclusive. Your notes are not a substitute for your own memory or that of other jurors. Instead, your verdict must result from the collective memory and judgment of all jurors based on the evidence and testimony presented during the trial.

At the conclusion of the trial, the bailiff will collect all of your notes and immediately destroy them. No one will ever read your notes.

In reaching your verdict, do not let bias, sympathy, prejudice, public opinion or any other sentiment for or against any party to influence your decision. Your verdict must be based on the evidence that has been received and the law on which I have instructed you.

Reaching a verdict is exclusively your job. I cannot participate in that decision in any way and you should not guess what I think your verdict should be from something I may have said or done. You should not think that I prefer one verdict over another. Therefore, in reaching your verdict, you should not consider anything that I have said or done, except for my specific instructions to you.

Pay careful attention to all the instructions that I gave you for that is the law that you must follow. You will have a copy of my instructions with you when you go to the jury room to deliberate. All the instructions are important and you must consider all of them together. There are no other laws that apply to this case and even if you do not agree with these laws, you must use them in reaching your decision in this case.

When you go to the jury room, the first thing you should do is choose a presiding juror. The presiding juror should see to it that your discussions are orderly and that everyone has a fair chance to be heard.

It is your duty to talk with one another in the jury room and to consider the views of all the jurors. Each of you must decide the case for yourself, but only after you have considered the evidence with the other members of the jury. Feel free to change your mind if you are convinced that your position should be different. You should all try to agree. But do not give up your honest beliefs just because the others think differently. Keep an open mind so that you and your fellow jurors can easily share ideas about the case.

I will give you a verdict form with questions you must answer. I have already instructed you on the law that you are to use in answering these questions. You must follow my instructions and the form carefully. You must consider each question separately. Please answer the questions in the order they appear. After you answer a question, the form tells you what to do next. I will now read the form to you: *(read form of verdict)*

Your verdict must be unanimous, that is, your verdict must be agreed to by each of you. When you are finished filling out the form, your presiding juror must write the date and sign it at the bottom. Return the form to the bailiff.

If any of you need to communicate with me for any reason, write me a note and give it to the bailiff. In your note, do not disclose any vote or split or the reason for the communication.

You may now retire to decide your verdict.

Special Verdict Form

VERDICT

We, the jury, return the following verdict:

1.   Was there negligence on the part of Defendant, RACHEL ROWE, which was a legal cause of damage to Plaintiff, JOHN DOE?

YES ____   NO ____

If your answer to question 1 is NO, your verdict is for the Defendant, and you should not proceed further, except to date and sign this verdict form and return it to the courtroom. If your answer to question 1 is YES, please answer question 2.

2.   Was there negligence on the part of Plaintiff, JOHN DOE, which was a legal cause of his damage?

YES ____   NO ____

If your answer to question 2 is YES, please answer question 3. If your answer to question 2 is NO, please skip question 3 and answer questions 4 and 5.

3.   State the percentage of negligence which was a legal cause of damage to Plaintiff, JOHN DOE, that you charge to:

RACHEL ROWE _____%

JOHN DOE   _____%

Total must be 100%

In determining the amount of any damages, do not make any reduction because of the negligence, if any, of Plaintiff, JOHN DOE. If you find Plaintiff, JOHN DOE, negligent in any degree, the court, in entering judgment, will reduce JOHN DOE'S total amount of damages (100%) by the percentage of negligence that you find was caused by JOHN DOE.

Please answer questions 4 and 5.

4.   What is the total amount of JOHN DOE'S damages for medical expenses incurred in the past, and medical expenses to be incurred in the future? $ _____

5.   What is the total amount of JOHN DOE'S damages for lost earnings in the past and loss of earning capacity in the future? $ _____

- 18 -

If the greater weight of the evidence shows that JOHN DOE'S injuries were in whole or in part permanent within a reasonable degree of medical probability, please answer question 6:

6. What is the total amount of JOHN DOE'S damages for pain and suffering, disability, physical impairment, disfigurement, mental anguish, inconvenience, aggravation of a disease or physical defect and loss of capacity for the enjoyment of life sustained in the past and to be sustained in the future? $ _____

TOTAL DAMAGES OF JOHN DOE
(add lines 1, 2, and, if applicable, 3) $ _____

SO SAY WE ALL, this _____ day of _____, 2 ___

_____
FOREPERSON

Revised November 21, 2013

The model instructions were retrieved from the Florida Supreme Court website located at the following web address:

http://www.floridasupremecourt.org/civ_jury_instructions/instructions.shtml.

Appendix II

POST-ACCIDENT CHECKLIST

- Stop vehicle

- Seek medical attention if needed

- Report accident

- Do *not* admit anything

- Obtain witnesses contact information

- Take photos

- Contact an attorney for advice (optional) [Q: why is this optional?]

- Call your insurance company (or attorney will)

- Call other driver's insurance company (or attorney will)

Appendix III

INFORMATION TO BRING TO ATTORNEY CHECKLIST

- Accident report

- Insurance policy

- Medical bills

- Physicians names that are treating you

- Correspondence between you and other parties

- Witnesses information

- Expenses that resulted from accident

- Photographs from accident scene

- Photographs of injuries

- Citations/legal notices

- Any notes/journal with notes to help your case

Appendix IV

SAMPLE NEW CLIENT QUESTIONNAIRE

Date of Intake:_____

Date of Incident:_____

Type of Incident:_____

SOL:_____
  (indicate what State if not FL)

THE FLORIDA LEGAL ADVOCACY GROUP, P.A.

Prior Lawyer: Y / N

Companion case: Y / N

Birthplace:_____
How Long in FL? _____

New Client information

Name: _____

Address:_____

City/St/Zip: _____

Referred by:_____

Emergency Contact: _____
      (name / addr / phone / relationship /email)
SS#: _____

Education: _____

Phone: _____

Phone: _____

Email: _____

DOB: _____

Ref'd to: _____

Spouse: _____

Photo Taken: Y / N

Convictions: Y / N _____

DESCRIPTION OF INCIDENT:_____

_____

_____

_____

_____

Medical Providers seen:

1._____   2. _____

  _____   _____

  _____   _____

3._____   4. _____

  _____   _____

  _____   _____

Vehicles involved:

CLIENT (vehicle client in)

Type of Vehicle: _____
(year / make / model / prior damage)

Owner / Driver of vehicle: _____

_____

Others in vehicle: _____

Plaintiff seated where: _____

Other vehicles in household:

_____

Photos taken: Y / N   Who to do: _____

Estimated Damage to Plaintiff's vehicle: _____

Insured by: _____

Claim/Policy#: _____
Owned by: _____

Adjuster:_____

Date Notified:_____

Limits: PIP:___ UM: ___ MP: ___
UM Rejected: Y / N / DK

Location of Vehicle: _____

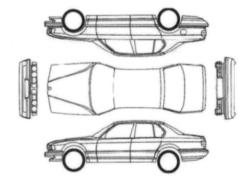

Responding Law Enforcement Agency: _____

Have Police Report: Y / N   Have Driver's Exchange Only: Y / N

                                             Police Report Done: Y / N

Vehicles involved: (cont'd)

DEFENDANT:

Type of Vehicle: _____
(year / make / model)

Driver of vehicle: _____
_____

Others in vehicle: _____

Defendant seated where: _____

Photos taken: Y / N

Insured by: _____

Claim/Policy#: _____

Owned by: _____

Adjuster: _____

Date Notified: _____

Limits: BI _____

Location of Vehicle: _____

Estimated Damage to Defendant's vehicle: _____

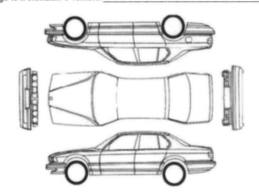

Employment:

Employer	Occupation	Dates employed	Rate of Pay

Lost time from work: Y / N   How Much: _____

Witnesses:

1. _____

2. _____

_____

_____

_____

_____

3. _____

4. _____

_____

_____

_____

_____

Prior Medical Care:

_____ Auto accident

_____ Workers Comp

_____ SSD

_____ Group Health

_____ Family Dr.

_____ Last Med Care b/4

_____ Pre-existing conditions

Injuries:

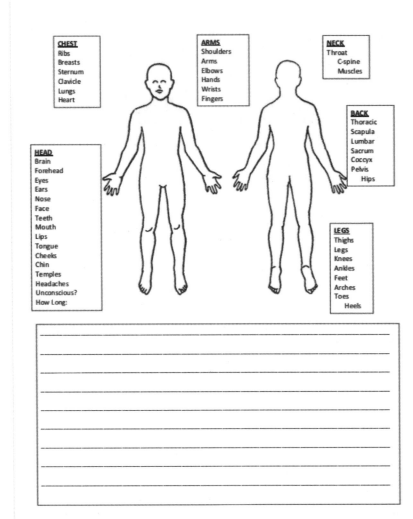

CHEST
Ribs
Breasts
Sternum
Clavicle
Lungs
Heart

ARMS
Shoulders
Arms
Elbows
Hands
Wrists
Fingers

NECK
Throat
  C-spine
  Muscles

BACK
Thoracic
Scapula
Lumbar
Sacrum
Coccyx
Pelvis
  Hips

HEAD
Brain
Forehead
Eyes
Ears
Nose
Face
Teeth
Mouth
Lips
Tongue
Cheeks
Chin
Temples
Headaches
Unconscious?
How Long:

LEGS
Thighs
Legs
Knees
Ankles
Feet
Arches
Toes
  Heels

NOTES ABOUT HOW INCIDENT EFFECTED CLIENT
(hobbies, activities, family events, work events, etc)

_____

Letters to Send Out:

___ 1. Thank you to client
___ 2. Notice to Defendant
___ 3. Notice to Defendant Carrier
___ 4. Notice to PIP/UM Carrier
___ 5. Request for wage information
___ 6. Notice to Gov't Entities
___ 7. Lien inquiry to health insurance
8. Lien inquiry to Medicare / Medicaid

Forms Signed:

___ 1. Retainer Agreement
___ 2. Statement of Client's Rights
___ 3. Authorization for Medical Recs
___ 4. Authorization for wage info
___ 5. PIP Application
___

What to Expect

According to The American Chiropractic Association (ACA), many people seeking medical treatment do not know what to expect during their first visit to a Chiropractor. The ACA website provides the following information to help new patients.

Chiropractors start by taking a patient's history and then performing a physical examination to develop a working diagnosis. Imaging or lab tests (such as MRI, CT scan or X-ray) may be used to confirm a diagnosis. The combination of the history, exam, and diagnostic studies will enable your doctor of chiropractic to reach a diagnosis, which will help him or her to determine whether chiropractic services are appropriate for your condition. If your doctor determines you would be more appropriately managed or co-managed by another health care professional, he or she will make the proper referral. Through a process of shared decision-making, you and your doctor will determine if chiropractic services are right for you. As part of this process, the doctor will explain your condition, recommend a treatment plan and review the risks and benefits of all procedures. Based on the extent, timing or severity of the patient's condition, chiropractic interventions may require several visits. Patients may also receive advice on home care, lifestyle modifications, exercise instruction and nutritional advice.

Source: The American Chiropractic Association (ACA), https://acatoday.org/Patients/Why-Choose-Chiropractic/What-to-Expect-on-Your-First-Visit

Social Media

The Florida Legal Advocacy Group

Attorney Stanley Plappert

Facebook

@TheFloridaLegalAdvocacyGroup

Twitter

@splappert

YouTube

The Florida Legal Advocacy Group

Doctor Appointment Mileage Log

NOTES

About the Author

Stanley W. Plappert serves families with their legal needs from his office in Ocala, Florida. Stan has a background in insurance, real estate and business management in addition to his legal education and experience. Stan was a founding member of the Florida Legal Advocacy Group, P.A.

Stan counsels families with personal injury cases and related issues. Stan's clients have included physicians, pharmacists, business owners, accountants, attorneys, as well as officers of public corporations. He has handled the affairs of many retired families and heirs as well.

Stan is a graduate of Illinois Wesleyan University, where he received a Bachelor's degree with a major in Business Administration. He received a

Masters' degree in Business Administration (MBA) from Illinois State University. Stan received his Juris Doctorate from Stetson University College of Law in Gulfport, Florida. He has studied extensively overseas, including studies in Denmark, Germany, Switzerland, The Netherlands, Argentina and the Cayman Islands.

Stan is married and he and his wife have four children. He is active in his church and a member of the Ocala Silver Springs Rotary Club.